SHANGHAI

SHANGHAI

Photography by Wang Gang Feng, Derek Allan,
Magnus Bartlett, Mary Beth Camp, Anthony Cassidy,
Han Wei, Dallas and John Heaton, Leong Ka Tai,
George Mitchell and David Thurston

Text by Ian Findlay

HARRAP COLUMBUS

Published by Harrap Limited
19—23 Ludgate Hill, London EC4M 7PD
and The Guidebook Company Limited,
The Penthouse, 20 Hollywood Road, Central,
Hong Kong

Text and captions by Ian Findlay

Photography by Wang Gang Feng with additional photographs by Derek Allan (17 bottom, 22, 23, 34 top left, 39, 43); Magnus Bartlett (16, 37 right, 42, 56 left, 60, 61 bottom left); Mary Beth Camp (2-3, 10-11, 29 right, 30, 31, 40 top, 44 bottom, 57, 58 top, 59, 68, 69, 70, 71, 72, 73, 77); Anthony Cassidy (19 top, 40 left, 55 right, 62 bottom); Han Wei, China Photo Library (78-79); D & J Heaton (75); Leong Ka Tai (76); Leong Ka Tai, The Stock House (5); George Mitchell (6-7, 20-21, 61 top); David Thurston (24-25, 49 top).

Designed by Joan Law Design & Photography
Colour separations by Rainbow Graphic Arts Co., Ltd.
Jacket colour separations by Sakai Lithocolour
Printed in Hong Kong

ISBN: 0-7471-0119-1

Title Spread
At dusk, as people stream across Suzhou Creek's numerous bridges and wander its narrow embankment streets, Shanghai's citiscape takes on an eerie glow. The barges that ply the Creek, which winds through the industrial heart of the city, are moored together for the night, leaving the waterway at its quietest.

Page 5
Neon signs on the spire of Da Shijie, the Great World entertainment centre.

Pages 6-7
Beginning as a muddy waterfront track, Shanghai's Bund quickly became the most famous and photographed avenue in the Far East. Here, in the late 1840s, the first foreign trading companies and consulates established their offices. Against the backdrop of solid colonial architecture, little changed in the past half-century, early morning taijiquan *experts twist and turn in slow and graceful movement.*

Pages 8-9
There are few cities in the world that can boast a street as crowded as Shanghai's Nanjing Road. Stretching five kilometres (three miles) from the Bund, the road is divided into two sections, east and west. Nanjing Road is a Chinese consumers' paradise. It has two of the nation's largest department stores, and more than 350 small shops selling everything from silk to tea. From early morning until evening, a constant sea of people floods the street, spilling over into the roads and slowing traffic to walking pace.

Pages 10-11
Bright, optimistic and colourful, the naive paintings of Shanghai's Jinshan County exude the spirit of post-Liberation China. This one is 'Watch Dragon Boats'.

Pages 12-13
An hour's drive from the bustling city centre, the rural life of Shanghai's ten metropolitan counties seems fixed in another, more peaceful age. The traditional method of carrying and transport — the bamboo pole and baskets — dominates the scene.

富力美
上海牌
大世界
游乐中心
GREAT WORLD
ENTERTAINMENT CENTRE

上海人参蜂皇浆
营养补品

钟表店
20
562FGP-032
T1029

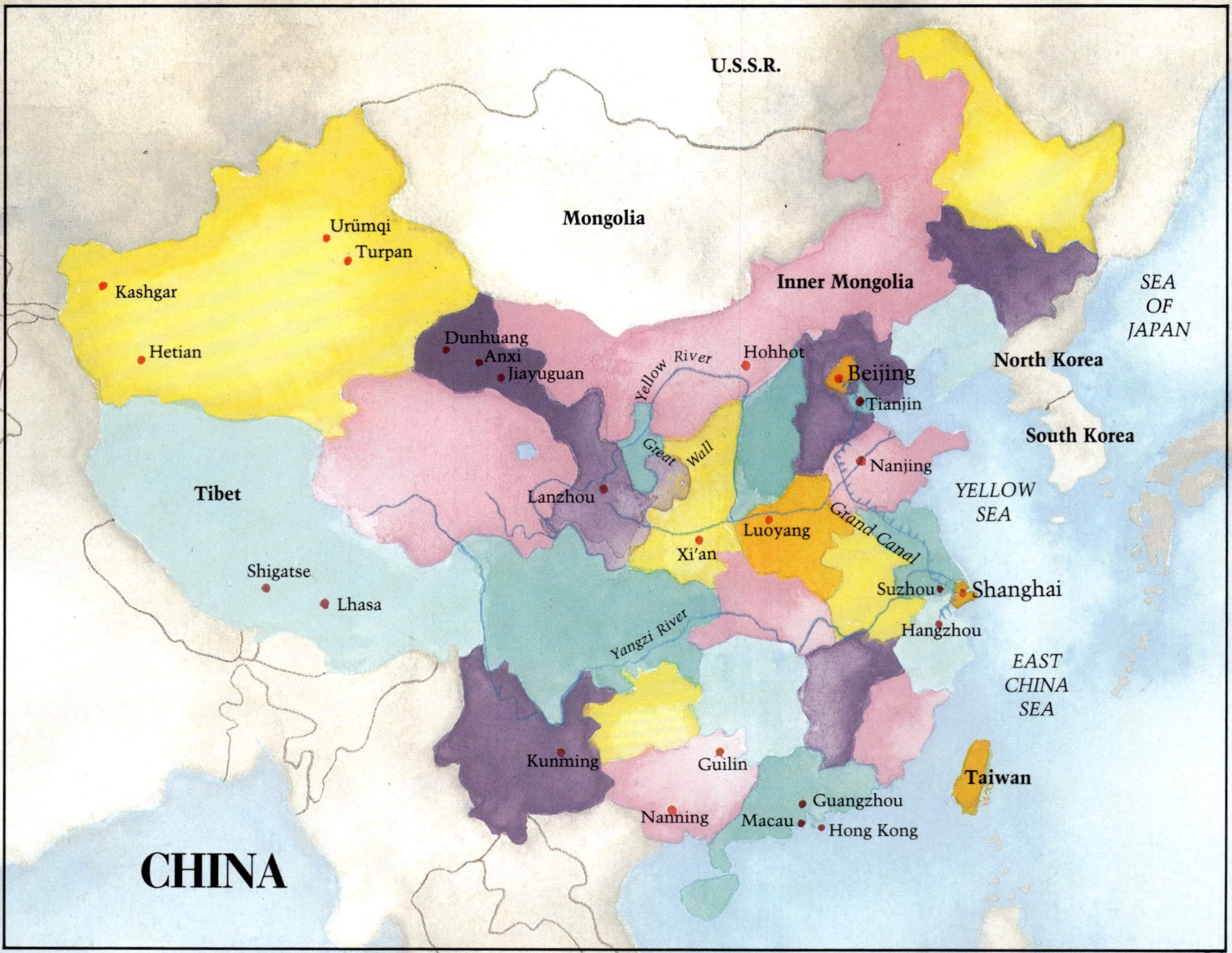
U.S.S.R.
Mongolia
Inner Mongolia
SEA OF JAPAN
North Korea
South Korea
YELLOW SEA
EAST CHINA SEA
Taiwan
Tibet
Urümqi
Turpan
Kashgar
Hetian
Dunhuang
Anxi
Jiayuguan
Yellow River
Hohhot
Beijing
Tianjin
Great Wall
Nanjing
Lanzhou
Grand Canal
Luoyang
Xi'an
Shigatse
Lhasa
Suzhou
Shanghai
Hangzhou
Yangzi River
Kunming
Guilin
Guangzhou
Nanning
Macau
Hong Kong
CHINA

INTRODUCTION

SHANGHAI, the 'City Above the Sea', once China's most cosmopolitan urban centre, dominates the country's eastern provinces. One of China's three great municipalities falling directly under the authority of the central government (the others being Beijing and Tianjin), Shanghai is tucked inland on the left bank of the Huangpu River some 20 kilometres (12 miles) from the Yangzi River delta.

The city's estimated current population of over 12 million lives in the municipality's 12 districts and ten surrounding counties; together they cover a total area of 6,185 square kilometres (2,387 square miles).

Shanghai has a tension and vitality, a sense of style and cultural diversity to its bustling everyday life that sets it apart from all other Chinese cities, even in this day of rapid modernization. Also, it remains the traditional industrial and commercial centre of modern China, and its contribution to the country's economy is enormous. In the early 1980s it produced one-sixth of the nation's state revenue, manufactured one-third of all China's exports, and accounted for one-eighth of the value of the country's gross industrial output value. The city has weathered the storms of war and political upheavals as few others have and remains at the forefront of China's development and modernizations programmes, though there are many who claim it is beginning to falter.

The massive colonial buildings along the waterfront (known as the Bund) and its principal streets suggest that the city clings to the past with a vengeance. Though such epithets as 'Paris of the East' and 'Paradise of Adventurers' no longer apply to contemporary Shanghai, the city remains fixed in the modern traveller's mind as a place of historical mystery and adventure.

The precise origins of Shanghai as an inhabited location, however, are uncertain. Nineteenth-century archaeological finds suggest that there was a primitive community already active here 6,000 years ago. But 1,000 years ago, it was still little more than a fishing village with a number of small trading ports scattered throughout the area. It was an unappealing place to China's rulers of the day; they felt it was too far from the seat of the central government to be of importance.

Shanghai's rivers and streams that had their origins in Lake Taihu near Suzhou (to the northeast of Shanghai), changed their courses frequently as a result of flooding and consequently altered the very nature of the area. As more land was reclaimed from the rivers, marshes and swamps, Shanghai grew and settled, slowly revealing its potential as an important and influential trading port.

The city was officially established in 1074 during the Northern Song Dynasty, became an official administrative town in 1267 and a county — under the Mongol Yuan Dynasty — in 1292, with an estimated population of 330,000. Fish, salt and rice as well as cotton and silk came to dominate its early trade.

Shanghai is still commonly known by another name, *Hu*, the name for a bamboo implement used locally for fishing. The name Shanghai, however, comes from the Shanghaipu River, a tributary of the Songjiang River which flows past the present-day Shiliupu Wharf where today's international passengers disembark from their liners.

Shanghai's reputation as a prosperous trading port and a centre of communications south of the Yangzi River quickly spread. Japanese and Korean merchants became prominent traders in the city. But in the 15th century, a new element arrived in Shanghai whose activities were to change the face of the city for the next 300 years — the pirate.

Japanese pirates, along with Korean and Chinese, raided the coast frequently. Their raids, at first haphazard, became increasingly organized and ferocious, until they came to dominate many of the sea lanes leading to the city. Japanese pirates disguised as merchants together with *ronin* (renegade samurai) met with little resistance initially as they moved up-river towards the city.

This imposing sculpture dominates the museum and tomb of Lu Xun (1881-1936) in Shanghai's Hongkou Park. The foremost author, essayist and critic of his day, he attacked social and political injustice without fear. Two of his masterpieces, A Madman's Diary, *the first colloquial (baihua) Chinese story published in modern China, and* The True Story of Ah Q, *were among those that earned him the kind of international reputation that no other Chinese writer has attained.*

It is estimated that there were 20,000 pirates active in and around Shanghai by the early 1550s. Their activities turned an open city into a closed one when it was decided to build a defensive wall around it. When eventually completed, the wall was five kilometres (three miles) long, over six metres (18 feet) high and five metres (15 feet) thick. It had 3,600 crenellations, six land gates and four water gates (each with a different name), five guard towers and 20 arrow towers for soldiers.

By 1560, the threat of pirates in Shanghai had vanished. The wall, surrounding what came to be known as the 'Native City', was demolished between 1912 and 1914.

Western trading companies, which had been forced by Imperial Edict to trade only from Macau and Canton, sought to expand their commercial interest along the China coast in the late 18th century. In 1756, under the orders of the British East India Company, a Mr Frederick Pigou visited Shanghai. He wrote favourably about the potential of the port but his report was ignored. Seventy-five years later, a second expedition was dispatched.

Desperate to expand their China trade and afraid for their trade monopoly at Canton, the British East India Company ordered Hugh Hamilton Lindsay and the German Lutheran missionary Karl Gutzlaff both on false papers to Shanghai. They sailed on the *Lord Amherst,* which had been secretly chartered from traders Dent and Company, and carried a cargo of British broadcloth, calico and cotton, but no opium.

Both men, though treated rudely by local officials, were impressed by what they saw. Lindsay, on his return, recommended Shanghai highly, considering it the best possible place from which to trade. 'I was so much struck with the vast quantity of junks entering the river that I caused them to be counted . . . . Upwards of 400 varying from 100 to 400 tons passed from Woosung to Shanghai,' Lindsay reported. Within seven years, under the Treaty of Nanking, Shanghai, as well as Amoy (Xiamen), Canton, Fuzhou and Ningbo, were opened to foreign trade.

The first foreign settlers lived in the old walled city and were something of a curiosity to the locals. But within a year, most of the small group of foreign residents had moved out. In 1843 there were a mere '23 foreign residents and families, the consular flag, 11 merchant houses and two Protestant missionaries'. Eighty years later, the foreign community of Shanghai had grown to number 2,405.

The symbols of foreign power were quickly established, as the Western style of work of one the city's earliest Chinese artists, Chou Kwa, shows. In 1857, there were 17 buildings on the Bund housing the offices of the leading European companies in the Far East and the consulates of half a dozen countries. One anonymous writer of the day was so impressed by the sturdiness of the buildings that he was moved to write that 'the residences of large British firms were successfully created in the style of mingled solidity and elegance which has almost entitled Shanghai to contest with Calcutta the designation of the City of Palaces'.

As the swamps and marshes were cleared, foreign control of the city became evident. All the concessions date from the 1840s, but while the French retained control over their concession as a separate entity, the British and Americans eventually joined forces and created what was to become known as the International Settlement in 1863, ruled over by a municipal council and a mixed court.

By the 1890s the foreign part of Shanghai was deemed a great success, while the old walled city remained a dark, squalid place. *Shen Pao*, the earliest Chinese newspaper in the city (launched in 1861) wrote that Shanghai from 'a miserable rustic area has become a market to which men of all nations hasten like rivers to the sea, and to which merchants come with no regard for distance. The streets are sprinkled and swept every day.'

But not everything appeared sparkling clean to visitors. At times, Shanghai, the Eastern Gateway to China, seemed like a lawless place. The city had become a haven for transients, drug-dealers, gamblers and adventurers who came for the easy money and easy living. Many stayed, of course, for here they were safe from most laws. Others, however, rolled 'up and down the Eastern World . . . making Shanghai their headquarters, owing to the fact that it is the land of no extradition', noted a turn-of-the-century American guide to the Orient.

The Shanghainese, considered cunning, shrewd, arrogant and boastful in turn by their fellow countrymen, had much to be proud of in their city. Far from being a backwater, in the international climate of the 19th century Shanghai moved along with the best of them.

By 1865, there were gas lamps on the streets and the city's first land cable had been laid from Shanghai to Wusong. The city's first telephone was used in 1881, and two years later piped water was introduced. The Yangshupu Power Station, China's first, quickly followed and led in turn to the growth of specialist factories in weaving, silk and papermaking. The first factory, the Jiangan Arsenal, was built in 1865 and began producing dynamite within a decade. By 1879, Shanghai had its first university, St John's College, while the first national university was opened in 1896; today it is known as Jiaotong (Communications) University. In the same year, China's largest publishing house, Commercial Press, was established in Shanghai.

Not everything, of course, has gone smoothly for Shanghai in its prosperity. Wars, invasions and riots were commonplace in the 19th century. First the Small Sword Society and the Taiping Rebels in the 1850s and 1860s threatened the safety of the city and resulted in the founding of the multinational Shanghai Volunteer Force in 1853. They were called out during the riots in the French Concession in 1874 and 1883 as well as during the Boxer Uprising in 1900. But the oddest ones the troops had to attend to were the Wheelbarrow Riots in 1897, when the Municipal Council attempted to increase the licence fees for wheelbarrows. These forced the Council to resign. Political and civilian unrest continued sporadically until the Sino-Japanese War of 1937-1945, but by then the heart of the 'Paris of the East' had been broken and within a few years the communist liberation of the city brought a century of foreign domination of the city to an end.

Though there are many other cities in China that have been significantly influenced by foreigners, Shanghai remains the most European city in the country. Until the 1920s Shanghai was a flat city architecturally, without any truly significant buildings beyond those on the Bund and a few others in outlying areas. The reason was quite simple: the ground was unstable. 'Engineers have bored 800 feet into the sub-soil of Shanghai, but have found no solid rock,' noted the *China Journal* for May 1930. It was also noted that the soil was practically 'liquid mud, and the buildings may be said to be floating'.

The 1920s and new engineering techniques which changed all that, also thrust Shanghai into a new period, and its most infamous one. Post-World War I Shanghai experienced an influx of adventurers, businessmen and refugees (Chinese, foreign and particularly Russian), the likes of which it had never seen before.

No matter who came, there seemed to be a place for them, and new hotels proliferated to meet the demand. The exclusive Burlington Hotel had complained in 1909 that it had to throw 'open its doors to the public'. The Palace Hotel (now a south wing of the Peace Hotel), which replaced the old Central Hotel on the corner of Nanjing Road and the Bund, was a lively place, always busy with the comings and goings of a hundred nationalities speaking a babel of tongues. But the two hotels that set the pace for extravagance in Shanghai were the Astor (now the Pujiang) and the Cathay (now the Peace).

The Cathay, at the corner of Nanjing Road and the Bund, was completed for the entrepreneur Victor Sassoon in 1929. As befitted the extravagance of the age, the hotel cost a staggering US$18 million to build. It boasted the finest of everything, from marble

Temples to two different eras. The Cathedral of St Ignatius (top) in Xujiahui, opened in 1910, is the city's largest Catholic church. In 1967, the imposing twin spires were destroyed by Red Guards, but the bell tower escaped their wrath. The spires were completely rebuilt by the mid-1980s and the church restored to its former grandeur.

The Shanghai Exhibition Centre (bottom), once called the Palace of Sino-Soviet Friendship, was built in 1955. Here, in the cavernous halls, local and foreign companies come to show off their wares at a wide variety of annual exhibitions.

There is no single face that typifies the Shanghainese. Since Shanghai was opened up to the West in 1943, Chinese from throughout the country have thronged to it. Today, young and old live and play in a city still quite Western in appearance, but to a profoundly Chinese rhythm.

baths that had silver taps to the luxurious penthouse apartment where Sassoon fêted his friends and admirers. It was in this hotel that Noel Coward wrote one of his most outstanding plays, *Private Lives*, in three days.

The Astor Hotel lost its ranking as Shanghai's leading hotel in the 1920s. Nevertheless it remained popular. The American bar, called the Astor Bar, was overseen by a tough American ex-sailor called Tug Wilson. Every morning from 11 o'clock to noon there would be a free lunch of sardines, sausages, sandwiches, cold ham, salted pork and beef. But one was expected to buy one's own beer.

During tea and dinner at the Astor there was music played by two all-Russian bands in formal dress. They played semi-classical tunes in the lobby and waltzes and foxtrots in the main ballroom. To the strains of 'Tears in My Eyes', 'Old Blue Heaven', and 'Five Foot Two and Eyes of Blue' the patrons would dance the night away.

Partying seemed to many outsiders to be the only activity of a significant portion of the population. 'There were parties at hotels every night, and you could go from one to the other and still be dancing at four o'clock in the morning', recalls the breezy voice of an old Shanghailander (as foreign settlers in Shanghai were known) on a sunny afternoon in Hong Kong half a century later. The long leisurely nights have gone. There are no longer Hawaiian tunes, waltzes, foxtrots, tangos or Charlestons played by such orchestras as Frank Casino's at the Metropole Garden and Ballroom or Henry Nathan's at the Cathay. Only at the Peace Hotel can the sounds of such ancients hits as 'Stormy Weather', 'Harbour Lights' and 'Chattanooga Choo Choo' still be heard. There are no longer any clubs like the Cercle Sportif Français, Del Monte's, the Casanova and Ciro's. But it seems appropriate that, 50 years on, Shanghai's nightlife still revolves around the hotels.

Today's Shanghai is a much sterner place, more frugal in every way. But it is still in many ways a city of adventurers. People continue to come here from China's other provinces looking for a different and better life.

Shanghai still has the finest shopping in the country along its major thoroughfares of Nanjing Road and Huaihai Road. The sophistication of its arts, music, ballet, opera, television, theatre and cinema attracts the restless spirits of the countryside who long for the bright lights and gaiety of the big city. And for the young who seek new heroes contemporary Shanghai has plenty of those, from the lithe models who stroll the catwalks at new fashion shows to the sporting heroes of volleyball, football, gymnastics and, increasingly, tennis.

But truly one of the great joys of Shanghai lies in its multitude of restaurants. There are over 600 restaurants specializing in all the major varieties of Chinese cuisine, from Cantonese to Sichuanese, from Pekingnese to Hunanese. Fresh and salt water fish, and particularly crab, are among the most tempting of dishes. But meat-eaters and vegetarians are also well catered for as are foreigners who prefer their own cuisine. There are now a number of smoky bars and restaurants as well as discotheques, where the young and the young-at-heart can enjoy an evening.

Physically, the city that the great modern Chinese writers such as Lu Xun, Mao Dun, Ai Qing and Ba Jin all knew, retains much of its old charm. While many of the more notorious and monstrous slums, the 'sore thumbs' of the past, have been torn down, there is still much to do.

Searching for the past in Shanghai is becoming increasingly difficult, if one ventures beyond the buildings of the Bund and the major streets. Luckily it is not yet impossible. The old city, though cleaner, is just as crowded. And it is there that one of Shanghai's most enduring monuments of the past, Yuyuan Garden, remains. Built between 1559 and 1577 for Pan Yunduan and restored in 1982, the garden covers an area of some 20,000 square metres (five acres). To walk here is to take a brief step back in time to a more gracious age. It is a place fit for contemplation and a haven from the bustle and crowded streets of the city.

Longhua Temple and Longhua Pagoda, said to have been built in 247 AD and reconstructed in 977, is a reminder that not all was destroyed during the Cultural Revolution (1966-76). The same is true of Square Pagoda and Screen Wall, constructed in the 11th and 14th centuries respectively.

But Shanghai, with 14 sister cities around the world, is not in the business of looking backward. Certainly it needs a facelift and above all some urban planning to alleviate the cramped, narrow streets. But what was once an inhospitable place with little apparent prospect of success, that nevertheless knew great prosperity in the last 100 years, is now rapidly again becoming one of the major cities of the world.

And it has every prospect of attaining this target. Shanghai faces stiff competition from other Chinese cities today and there are those who have many doubts about the city's ability to regain its former position of glory and power. But the Shanghainese, with their entrepreneurial skill and flair that is the envy of the nation, have the resilience necessary for great achievements.

Preceding page
Under a clear blue sky Shanghai's low cityscape meanders into the distance. Shanghai Mansions and the Russian Consulate (bottom right) dominate Waibaidu Bridge and the confluence of Suzhou Creek and the Huangpu River. Across the bridge are the tree-covered grounds of the former British Consulate (bottom left).

Two women (left) share a private, humorous moment, while a bargeman (right) poles his load of gravel along Suzhou Creek.

Preceding page
From the vantage point of Shanghai's television tower, the city's brown patchwork of buildings old and new stretches into the horizon. With more than seven million people living in an urban area of only 340 square kilometres (131 square miles), Shanghai is one of the most crowded areas on earth.

Left and above
The most popular way to relieve the tensions of the city is the variant forms of taijiquan. *Early morning in the city's streets, parks and courtyards sees thousands of Shanghai's citizens moving in deep concentration through the complex routines of the exercise. In the past decade, however, Shanghai's youth has turned increasingly to modern sports, from volleyball to tennis, from gymnastics to swimming. But wherever there are athletes there are always spectators who simply stand and stare.*

Once considered a luxury, the bicycle is now ubiquitous on the city's streets. And with it traffic chaos has come to the streets that seems, at times, to have a will and a momentum of its own.

飞乐音响公司
延中实业公司
爱使电子公司
市工商银行债券
卖出
最高价
最低价

Capitalist ways have again come to Shanghai with the reopening of the Shanghai Stock Exchange. Dealing in shares of only four companies, and using an abacus to check calculations, the director (left) fulfills a role which is a far cry from that of his counterparts abroad. But high-tech is making inroads into Shanghai's office life (above). These two young women are employees at the Shanghai branch of China's leading computer company.

KAIGE

In the past five years, Shanghai's city government has built a number of overpasses for safety and to help ease the push of pedestrian traffic. This circular overpass (left) is dominated by the bulk of the Number One Department Store. The overpasses are occasionally used as viewing platforms by visitors and residents alike. Jinling Road (above) in downtown Shanghai, though not as crowded as many other streets, has its fair share of traffic congestion. The slogans on the pillars of the covered sidewalk are advertising everything from office products and leather goods to electrical appliances.

Shanghai has a good number of official markets with controlled prices and a limited range of goods. In the past five years, with the relaxation of economic regulations, however, entrepreneurs have opened up free markets where peasants can sell their own produce, from fresh milk and eggs to fruit and vegetables, for much higher prices (left). The slogan in red (above) exhorts 'everyone to work together to create a fine, healthy environment'.

上海牌蚊香三星牌高级蚊香
飞鹰牌刀片
GREAT WORLD
ENTERTAINMENT CENTRE
发扬精神文明，积极参加卫生劳动

A Shanghai fireman, in his bright red truck, smiles on his way to work (above). The Great World (left) epitomized all that was sordid in old Shanghai. Filled with singsong girls, gambling tables, acrobats, actors, pimps and much else besides, the Great World drew the innocent and the gullible, the crooked and the vile, in search of adventure and a living. Today, the complex is referred to as a Youth Palace and the crowds that throng the place are offered entertainment more innocent than the sort their grandparents knew.

Food and moments of quiet contemplation seem almost obsessions in Shanghai. Both are taken with the utmost seriousness.

Not so far from the madding crowd (right) small-time entrepreneurs (left and above) sell biscuits and sunglasses and repair shoes, while a young man reads a group of film posters advertising some of China's new film productions.

维护社会公德
保持市容整洁

争分夺秒 奔向2000！

Beneath a giant poster exhorting all Chinese to make 'every second and minute count in the race toward the year 2000' (left), groups of children play. A snappily dressed young couple stroll unconcernedly by a poster which extols the virtues of the one-child family.

China's one-child family policy has led to better overall child care. But already at home and in school adults are complaining that the single children of the post-Mao period, always the centre of attention, are now thoroughly spoiled.

Shanghai's inner city housing problems are acute. Many buildings are dilapidated and the authorities acknowledge that they should be condemned. But they are home to millions and the Shanghainese bravely make the most of it.

In contrast to the almost shantytown feel to the inner city dwellings, these houses suggest a past world of splendour, wealth, ease and comfort.

Teahouses, like the Huxinting (left) in the old town next to the Yu Garden, are old favourites with the Shanghainese. The story-tellers who frequented these places in the past are now enjoying a comeback. An elderly soldier enjoys a joke and a cigarette (right).

The park is a refuge from the crush of the city. Lovers, absorbed in each other, ignore the world; old friends joke and chat; and the solitary reader is lost in his book. But whatever is happening there is always a photographer (right) around to capture the scene.

海鷗

供应時间
-1.30
7.30

The pressure to marry is as strong in China today as it has always been. (Left) The bride's popular traditional dress is something that has only recently reappeared in Shanghai. (Above and right) Children in their Sunday best in Renmin Park.

Father and son on a winter day (above).

Two Chinese sailors on shore leave (left).

In the past five years, private street markets have sprung up in just about every city district. The man and his daughter (right) own a stall at the clothes market in Huating. The colourful clothes on the racks beside them are a far cry from the standard greens and blues of the Maoist era.

Since the first Western missionaries settled in Shanghai in the 1840s, both Catholicism and Protestantism have been deeply rooted in the community. The International Church on Hengshan Road (above) is a popular place of worship for Chinese and foreigners alike. In a quiet, candle-lit corner of the Catholic Cathedral, an elderly Shanghainese has a personal moment of contemplation. To meet a rising demand for religious texts, the four Protestant lay people (right) have translated the Bible into modern simplified Chinese characters.

聖哉 聖哉 聖哉

The eight-sided, seven-storeyed Longhua Pagoda (left), first built in AD 174 and rebuilt during the Song Dynasty (960-1279), continues to attract hundreds of thousands of tourists a year. An elderly craftsman lovingly helps to restore a damaged temple wall (above). The symbols of two eras (right) stand in stark contrast.

Tucked away amidst the urban sprawl of the northwest of the city stands the Temple of the Jade Buddha, built between 1911 and 1918. Famous for its two jade images of Buddha and a complete set of the Buddhist canon printed in 1890, the temple offers the visitor one of the more interesting sights in Shanghai. The complex of buildings was recently renovated and this has made it easier for the temple's monks and worshippers to go about their business.

There have been parks in Shanghai since the late 1850s. Many of the city's parks began life as private gardens of the wealthy and were opened to the public after 1949. Some of the gardens are simple affairs while others offer a landscape of intricate rockeries, ponds and architecture from a more leisurely time (left). The bedroom (above) is in the traditional style with the furniture in heavy woods, the bed enclosed and the wall hung with scroll paintings and calligraphy.

Qingpu County, 23 kilometres (14 miles) west of Shanghai, was a prosperous market and shipping area from the Tang Dynasty (618-907), but after the end of the Song Dynasty (960-1127) the area was neglected as a business centre. Today, besides being the main provider of fresh-water fish for Shanghai, it is a popular tourist spot. The old rural ways of the canals and the fields are still much in evidence.

真 执 行

The wealth of the city is not evenly reflected in the countryside. Here (left) an old man waits patiently for someone to buy his sugar-cane. The tradition of bundling children up in layers of clothing against the cold (above) is still much in evidence in the countryside.

Cao Xiuwen (left) and Zhang Xingying (above) are just two of the many peasants active in Jinshan's naive-painting circles. The paintings are characterized by their bold, bright colours depicting everything from home life and leisure to work in the fields and the rivers. The dominant themes of the works are optimism and abundance.

More than half-a-dozen styles of opera, ranging from the formal Peking Opera to Huju, Shanghai's own style of opera, are performed by Shanghai's professional opera troupes. The correct application of the makeup which fixes each character within the plot is absolutely vital. It is a delicate task and it requires years of training and practice to become accomplished. Though traditional opera fell foul of the authorities during the Cultural Revolution (1966-76), it has made a strong comeback in the city.

One of the most popular and accessible of Chinese operas is Yueju, or Shaoxing Opera. The style and form of this opera date from the early 20th century and come from the town of Shaoxing in Jiangsu. Shaoxing Opera has many similarities with modern theatre and was heavily influenced by the Chinese intellectuals of the May Fourth Movement of 1919. It is a pleasant form of opera, simple in design, easier on the ear than Peking Opera and often very amusing. No-one has to be an expert to enjoy it.

Right
Acrobats have always been a popular form of entertainment in China. The Shanghai Acrobatic Troupe is one of the best groups in the country and is world renowned for its versatility, power and sheer skill.

A young family window shops by night.

Not an uncommon sight today in Shanghai, the motorcycle has added greatly to the traffic congestion and the danger of crossing the street.

Following page
The Bund and Huangpu Park.

咖啡饮料
酒家
营业时间
TR